MW01679819

JUMP

JOURNAL FOR UNDERSTANDING MATHEMATICAL PRINCIPLES

Teacher's Edition

Eliza Akana

Jonelle Flight

Suzanne Forbes

Ann Watanabe

Common Core Education, Inc.

Maui, Hawaii

2nd Edition

No part of this publication may be reproduced, stored in a retrieval system, or transmitted in any form or by any means, electronic, mechanical, photocopying, recording, or otherwise, without the written permission of the publisher. For information regarding permission, write to Common Core Education, Inc., 1695 Olinda Road, Makawao, Maui, HI 96768

Second Edition

ISBN-13: 9780615814513

ISBN-10: 0615814514

Text copyright © 2011, 2013 by Common Core Education, Inc. All rights reserved.

Printed in the United States of America

Common Core State Standards for Mathematics © Copyright 2010. National Governors Association Center for Best Practices and Council of Chief State School Officers. All rights reserved.

Cover design by Jessica Matsumoto

Asking a student to understand something means asking a teacher to assess whether the student has understood it. But what does mathematical understanding look like? One hallmark of mathematical understanding is the ability to justify, in a way appropriate to the student's mathematical maturity, why a particular statement is true or where a mathematical rule comes from. Mathematical understanding and procedural skill are equally important, and both are assessable using mathematical tasks of sufficient richness.

-Common Core State Standards Initiative, 2010

Introduction to JUMP

How is JUMP aligned to the Common Core State Standards for Mathematics?

One of the major shifts in the Common Core State Standards (CCSS) for Mathematics is the call for rigor. JUMP is designed to meet the rigor of the standards by focusing on students' conceptual understanding and application of the mathematical principles. The authors have analyzed and interpreted each standard to provide journal prompts that reflect what students need to know and be able to do at each grade level. A CCSS information table is provided for each prompt in the Teacher's Edition. (See example below)

How does JUMP address the Critical Areas for each grade level?

The authors have identified Standards we believe address grade level Critical Areas. These Standards are highlighted in the CCSS information tables in the Teacher's Edition. (See example below)

→ Common Core State Standards for Mathematics 5.MD.3.a	
Grade:	5
Domain:	Measurement and Data
Cluster:	Geometric measurement: understand concepts of volume and relate volume to multiplication and to addition.
Standard:	Recognize volume as an attribute of solid figures and understand concepts of volume measurement. a. A cube with side length 1 unit, called a "unit cube," is said to have "one cubic unit" of volume, and can be used to measure volume.

Each student edition also includes prompts for content vocabulary terms that are essential to understanding mathematical concepts at each grade level. The terms that support the grade level Critical Areas identified by the CCSS and are highlighted, as well.

How does JUMP support the Standards for Mathematical Practice?

JUMP deepens students' understanding of mathematical concepts while reinforcing critical processes and proficiencies outlined in the CCSS Standards for Mathematical Practice. JUMP asks students to make sense of problems and persevere in solving them, reason abstractly and quantitatively, construct arguments and critique their work and the work of others, model with mathematics, and use mathematical tools. Most importantly, JUMP asks students to attend to precision while communicating mathematically.

© Common Core Education, Inc.

How is JUMP different from a workbook?

JUMP is designed to support the rigor of CCSS by promoting a deep conceptual understanding of mathematical concepts and principles. For example, a student may be able to mentally multiply 6 x 7, but he or she may not be able to explain the concept of multiplication. Unlike workbooks, which are designed for skills practice, JUMP is designed for understanding.

How often should I use JUMP?

It is recommended that students respond to journal prompts on a regular basis. The frequency of use will depend on the standards that have been taught.

How can JUMP be used?

JUMP can be used in a variety of settings:

- Whole group instruction
- Small group instruction
- Peer learning teams
- Partners
- Individually

JUMP can be used for a variety of purposes:

- Pre-assessment
- Formative assessment
- Summative assessment
- Guided practice
- Independent practice
- Homework
- Enrichment
- Intervention
- Evidence for parent/teacher conferences
- Evidence for portfolios

JUMP can be used by a variety of educators:

- General Education Teachers
- Special Education Teachers
- Teachers of English Language Learners
- Math Resource Teachers
- Summer School Teachers
- Intervention Teachers
- Tutors

© Common Core Education, Inc.

Tips for Using JUMP

Introducing JUMP to Your Students

Explain the purpose of JUMP to your students. "Math journals are used to show and tell our understanding of math. In our journal, we will draw, write, and explain our thinking. Each journal page has a prompt which we will use to guide our thinking and show what we have learned. Sometimes we might respond to prompts as a class. Sometimes we might respond in a small group or with a partner. And sometimes you will respond to a prompt on your own."

Introducing Important Elements: Signal Words

Explain to students that Signal Words are written in color to alert them that a task must be performed. Introduce the Signal Words and provide explanations and examples.

Draw:	Draw a picture or a model
Label:	Give a name to something you have drawn or written
Write:	Write words or numbers
Solve:	Find the solution or the answer
Explain:	Put your thinking into complete sentences
Measure:	Use a math measuring tool
Evaluate:	Find the numerical value
Plot:	Locate a point on a number line or coordinate plane

Grades 1-3: Signal Words are written in color in the prompt to alert students that a task must be performed. These words also are included in corresponding color-coded response boxes.

Grade 4-5: Signal Words are written in color in the prompt to alert students that a task must be performed. There are corresponding color-coded response boxes, but at these grade levels the Signal Words are not in the boxes.

© Common Core Education, Inc.

Introducing Important Elements: Efficient Drawings

As students progress through **JUMP**, the value of the numbers will increase. Drawing and representing larger numbers may become more difficult for students. We recommend teaching students to draw or represent numbers in the most efficient way. To do this, it may be helpful to use the following models:

Ones Dots: · · · · ·

Five dots = five ones or 5

Tens Sticks: | | | |

Four tens sticks = four tens or 40

Hundreds Squares: □ □ □

Three hundreds squares = three hundreds or 300

Example: 254 would be drawn like this:

□ □ | | | | | · · · ·

Introducing Important Elements: Defining Content Vocabulary

JUMP includes content vocabulary terms necessary for deep understanding of mathematical concepts at each level. Most of these terms support the grade level critical areas identified by CCSS.

Each term can be defined in slightly different ways. We feel that it is important for the teacher to define the term as it is used in your classroom. Teachers should provide a student-friendly definition and explicit instruction to build understanding of the term.

© Common Core Education, Inc.

General Directions for JUMP

The introduction of journal prompts will vary depending on your instructional purpose. If prompts are being used for formal assessment (pre-assessment, formative assessment, summative assessment, etc.), provide a minimal, yet consistent explanation. If prompts are being used for practice, more teacher guidance and explanation is appropriate.

Student understanding of grade-level content vocabulary for mathematics is also important. Content vocabulary prompts should be used as ongoing review. In keeping with the focus and coherence of CCSS, some content vocabulary may span across multiple grade levels.

Presenting a JUMP Prompt

Before:	Differentiate based on student needs
During:	Circulate to ensure students are engaged
After:	Review and assess student work

General Teaching Procedures

1. Read the prompt with the students or have students read the prompt independently.
2. Check for understanding by asking and answering questions using active participation procedures (e.g., partner sharing, choral responses).
3. Talk about the Signal Words.
4. If necessary, model how to answer the prompt following these procedures for effective instruction:

Model (I do it)	"My turn."
Lead or Prompt (We do it)	"Let's do this together."
Test or Check (You do it)	"Your turn."

JUMP as a Tool for Formative Assessment

JUMP is designed to support the implementation of the powerful practices that truly define formative assessment. The authors of JUMP understand that in order to reap the benefits of formative assessment, the students must have an active role in understanding what they are learning, where they are in the learning process, and what they can do to improve.

JUMP provides students the opportunity to practice and make corrections during their learning, receive feedback, and engage in reflection and self-assessment. Engaging students in the formative process also supports the Standards for Mathematical Practice.

© Common Core Education, Inc.

Scoring JUMP as a Class

Note: Set expectations for sharing student work and maintaining a respectful and positive learning environment. Follow procedures for explicit instruction when scoring journals as a class. Use active participation strategies (e.g. choral responses, partners) to keep students engaged.

Model (I do it): Whole Group

1. Select a student journal prompt to score with the class. You may delete the student's name.
2. Place the journal prompt on a document projector so that all students can see the prompt. (If a document projector is not available, you may copy the student's journal prompt onto an overhead transparency.)
3. Ask students to read the journal prompt chorally.
4. Focus on one task or section at a time.
5. Identify and discuss the scoring criteria of the task or section using the corresponding page in the Teacher's Edition.
6. Model the scoring process for your students by thinking out loud. Share your thoughts with students through each step as you look at the student example.
7. Score another student example of the journal prompt following the same procedures. Scoring at least two examples of the prompt is recommended to ensure that students understand the scoring procedures. Be sure to continue modeling your thinking process with each example.

Lead (We do it): Whole Group and Partners

8. Display another student example of the journal prompt and have students read the response to the first task or section. Ask students to discuss with their partners whether they would give credit for the response or not. They must be able to explain why they gave credit or why they chose not to give credit.
9. Call on individual students (or partners) to share their decision with the class.
10. Open the discussion so that other students may share their reasoning. At this point, don't give feedback. Let the students engage in an open class discussion to promote problem solving and higher level thinking. If they are able to accurately score someone else's journal prompt response, they are more likely to do well when responding to their own. (Teacher scaffolding, support, and feedback, will vary depending on the age of the students.)
11. Share your score and rationale with students.
12. Continue this process using another student example. Repeat until students are firm with the process. Initially, this could occur over several days. As students practice and as the prompts change, instructional time spent on understanding the scoring criteria will either decrease or increase.

© Common Core Education, Inc.

Check (You do it): Partners or Individuals

13. Decide which of the following options is appropriate for your class: (1) Students may trade journals with their partners and score each other's journal prompt response. Use this process every few journal prompts to encourage accountability, cooperative learning, self-assessment, and reflection. (2) Students may score their own journal prompts and write a reflective comment about what they did well and what they could improve on next time.

Be sure to model appropriate comments for your students. Examples include: "I answered all parts of the prompt completely." "My explanation was thorough." "My drawing of the model was appropriate." "I missed one part of the prompt because I did not read it carefully." Etc.

When students score prompts as a class, they engage in several formative practices, such as: using samples of student work to strengthen understanding, giving and receiving peer feedback, and self assessment.

Using the Self Assessment and Peer Feedback Section:

This section asks students to either self assess or receive peer feedback on their work. If a student is self assessing, the student will identify his or her own "JUMPS" (what went well) and his or her own "BUMPS" (what needs improvement). Next, the student will circle the appropriate face icon to indicate if his or her work demonstrates understanding, if he or she made mistakes but knows how to fix them, or if he or she needs help.

If students are receiving peer feedback, the peer will write his or her name. The peer will critique the work and identify the "JUMPS" and "BUMPS." The peer will then return the written feedback to the student, and the student will circle the appropriate face icon to indicate if his or her work demonstrates understanding, if he or she made mistakes but knows how to fix them, or if he or she needs help. Effective self-assessment and peer feedback require explicit instruction. Students need to see the process modeled and need to be involved in many guided practice opportunities before self-assessing and providing peer feedback independently.

Using the Strategy Toolbox Section:

The Strategy Toolbox is designed to have students create a collection of the most efficient strategies they have learned. Teachers need to be selective about the strategies that students are taught, because students will effectively use the strategies with which they are most comfortable. Students write the strategy, draw a representation of the strategy, and explain how the strategy helps them to solve problems. They can also tally how often they have used the strategy.

Through the use of the Strategy Toolbox, students are engaged in metacognition. They will recognize when and how to appropriately apply strategies they have learned and how the effective use of these strategies supports their learning.

© Common Core Education, Inc.

Bob gave each of three friends 5 apples and 10 oranges. How many pieces of fruit did he give them in all?

Write an expression. **Evaluate** the expression.

CCSS.5.OA.1—A 1

1 Point

Answers will vary.

Example: 3 x (5 + 10)

1 Point

25 pieces of fruit

Answer must be labeled.

Total = 2 Points

© Common Core Education, Inc.

Common Core State Standards for Mathematics 5.OA.1	
Grade:	5
Domain:	Operations and Algebraic Thinking
Cluster:	Write and interpret numerical expressions.
Standard:	Use parentheses, brackets, or braces in numerical expressions, and evaluate expressions with these symbols.

$\{3 + [(5 + 31) \div 6]\} \times 2$

Evaluate the expression. **Explain** the steps you used to evaluate the expression.

<u>1 Point</u>

18

<u>1 Point</u>

Answers will vary. Student's explanation must be accurate and complete.

2 CCSS.5.OA.1—B

Total = 2 Points

Common Core State Standards for Mathematics 5.OA.1	
Grade:	5
Domain:	Operations and Algebraic Thinking
Cluster:	Write and interpret numerical expressions.
Standard:	Use parentheses, brackets, or braces in numerical expressions, and evaluate expressions with these symbols.

© Common Core Education, Inc.

4 x (73,102 + 834)

Explain your interpretation of the expression.

CCSS.5.OA.2 3

1 Point

Answers will vary. Student's explanation must be accurate and complete.

Total = 1 Point

© Common Core Education, Inc.

Common Core State Standards for Mathematics 5.OA.2	
Grade:	5
Domain:	Operations and Algebraic Thinking
Cluster:	Write and interpret numerical expressions.
Standard:	Write simple expressions that record calculations with numbers, and interpret numerical expressions without evaluating them. *For example, express the calculation "add 8 and 7, then multiply by 2" as 2 x (8 + 7). Recognize that 3 x (18932 + 921) is three times as large as 18932 + 921, without having to calculate the indicated sum or product.*

Write a numerical pattern. **Explain** the rule for the pattern.

1 Point

Answers will vary.

1 Point

Answers will vary. Student's explanation must be accurate and complete.

Write a different numerical pattern. **Explain** the rule for the pattern.

1 Point

Answers will vary but must be different from the first pattern..

1 Point

Answers will vary. Student's explanation must be accurate and complete.

Write four ordered pairs using your first pattern for the *x* coordinates and your second pattern for the *y* coordinates.

1 Point

Answers will vary.

(This prompt is continued on the next page.)

Common Core State Standards for Mathematics 5.OA.3	
Grade:	5
Domain:	Operations and Algebraic Thinking
Cluster:	Analyze patterns and relationships.
Standard:	Generate two numerical patterns using two given rules. Identify apparent relationshps between corresponding terms. Form ordered pairs consisting of corresponding terms from the two patterns, and graph the ordered pairs on a coordinate plane. *For example, given the rule "Add 3" and the starting number 0, and given the rule "Add 6" and the starting number 0, generate terms in the resulting sequences, and observe that the terms in one sequence are twice the corresponding terms in the other sequence. Explain informally why this is so.*

© Common Core Education, Inc.

Draw a coordinate grid and label the x-axis and y-axis. **Plot** the points for your ordered pairs.

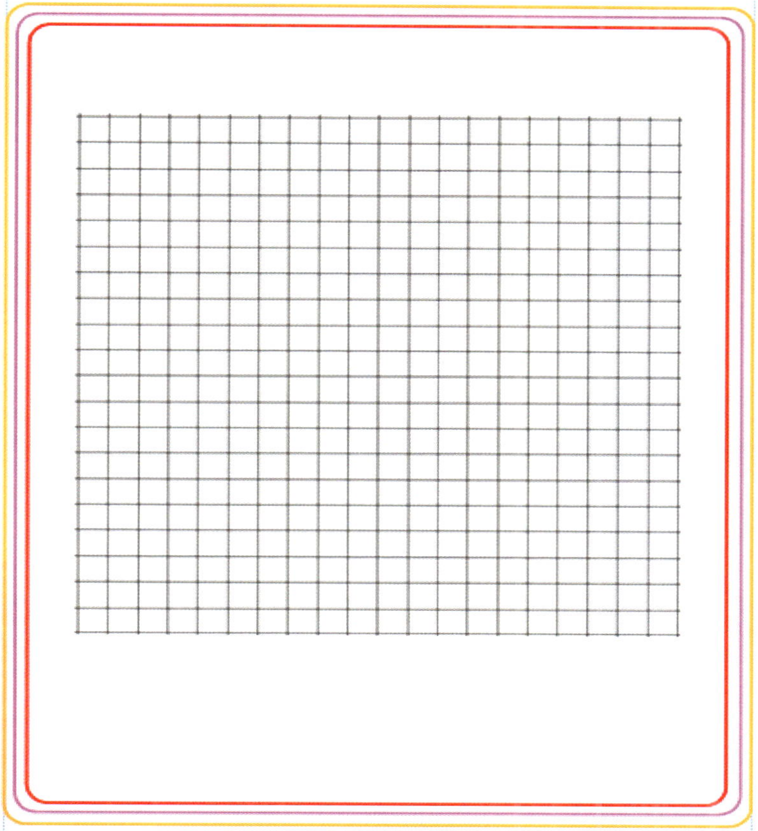

CCSS.5.OA.3 (Page 2 of 2) 5

<u>1 Point</u>

Student's coordinate grid must be accurate and complete and include labels for the x-axis and the y-axis.

<u>1 Point</u>

Answers will vary. Student accurately plots the points.

Total = 7 Points

Common Core State Standards for Mathematics 5.OA.3	
Grade:	5
Domain:	Operations and Algebraic Thinking
Cluster:	Analyze patterns and relationships.
Standard:	Generate two numerical patterns using two given rules. Identify apparent relationshps between corresponding terms. Form ordered pairs consisting of corresponding terms from the two patterns, and graph the ordered pairs on a coordinate plane. *For example, given the rule "Add 3" and the starting number 0, and given the rule "Add 6" and the starting number 0, generate terms in the resulting sequences, and observe that the terms in one sequence are twice the corresponding terms in the other sequence. Explain informally why this is so.*

© Common Core Education, Inc.

Write a five-digit number that includes values in the tenths and hundredths places. **Explain** the value of each digit using multiplication or division and your knowledge of the place value system.

6 CCSS.5.NBT.1

<u>1 Point</u>

Answers will vary but must include value in the tenths and hundredths places.

<u>1 Point</u>

Answers will vary. Student's explanation must show an understanding of the place value system.

Total = 2 Points

Common Core State Standards for Mathematics 5.NBT.1	
Grade:	5
Domain:	Number and Operations in Base Ten
Cluster:	Understand the place value system.
Standard:	Recognize that in a multi-digit number, a digit in one place represents 10 times as much as it represents in the place to its right and 1/10 of what it represents in the place to its left.

© Common Core Education, Inc.

Write a five-digit number. **Solve** for the product of your number and 10. **Solve** for the product of your number and 100. **Solve** for the product of your number and 1000. **Explain** the pattern in the number of zeros in the product when multiplying by powers of 10.

CCSS.5.NBT.2—A 7

1 Point

Answers will vary.

1 Point

Answers will vary.

1 Point

Answers will vary.

1 Point

Answers will vary.

1 Point

Answers will vary. Student's explanation must show an understanding of the place value system.

Total = 5 Points

Common Core State Standards for Mathematics 5.NBT.2	
Grade:	5
Domain:	Number and Operations in Base Ten
Cluster:	Understand the place value system.
Standard:	Explain patterns in the number of zeros of the product when multiplying a number by powers of 10, and explain patterns in the placement of the decimal point when a decimal is multiplied or divided by a power of 10. Use whole-number exponents to denote powers of 10.

© Common Core Education, Inc.

Write a five-digit number. Solve for the quotient of your number and 10. Solve for the quotient of your number and 100. Solve for the quotient of your number and 1000. Explain the pattern in the number of zeros in the quotient when dividing by powers of 10.

8 CCSS.5.NBT.2—B

1 Point

Answers will vary.

1 Point

Answers will vary.

1 Point

Answers will vary.

1 Point

Answers will vary.

1 Point

Answers will vary. Student's explanation must show an understanding of the place value system.

Total = 5 Points

Common Core State Standards for Mathematics 5.NBT.2	
Grade:	5
Domain:	Number and Operations in Base Ten
Cluster:	Understand the place value system.
Standard:	Explain patterns in the number of zeros of the product when multiplying a number by powers of 10, and explain patterns in the placement of the decimal point when a decimal is multiplied or divided by a power of 10. Use whole-number exponents to denote powers of 10.

© Common Core Education, Inc.

Write a five-digit number that includes value in the thousandths place using base-ten numerals. **Write** your number name. **Write** your number in expanded form. **Explain** how you know the value of each digit.

CCSS.5.NBT.3.a 9

1 Point

Answers will vary.

1 Point

Answers will vary.

1 Point

Answers will vary.

1 Point

Answers will vary. Student's explanation must show an understanding of the place value system.

Total = 4 Points

© Common Core Education, Inc.

Common Core State Standards for Mathematics 5.NBT.3.a	
Grade:	5
Domain:	Number and Operations in Base Ten
Cluster:	Understand the place value system.
Standard:	Read, write, and compare decimals to the thousandths. a. Read and write decimals to thousandths using base-ten numerals, number names, and expanded form, e.g., 347.392 = 3 x 100 + 4 x 10 + 7 x 3 + 3 x (1/10) + 9 x (1/100) + 2 x (1/1000).

Write two different decimal numbers using base-ten numerals. **Write** a symbol to compare your two numbers. **Explain** how you compared the numbers using your knowledge of base ten.

10 CCSS.5.NBT.3.b

1 Point

Answers will vary.

1 Point

Answers will vary. Student's explanation must show an understanding of place value and base ten.

Total = 2 Points

Common Core State Standards for Mathematics 5.NBT.3.b	
Grade:	5
Domain:	Number and Operations in Base Ten
Cluster:	Understand the place value system.
Standard:	Read, write, and compare decimals to the thousandths. b. Compare two decimals to thousandths based on meanings of the digits in each place, using >, =, and < symbols to record the results of comparisons.

© Common Core Education, Inc.

Write a decimal number that includes value in the thousandths place.
Explain how you would round your number to the nearest tenth.
Explain how you would round your number to the nearest hundredth.

CCSS.5.NBT.4 11

1 Point

Answers will vary.

1 Point

Answers will vary. Student's explanation must be accurate and complete.

1 Point

Answers will vary. Student's explanation must be accurate and complete.

Total = 3 Points

© Common Core Education, Inc.

Common Core State Standards for Mathematics 5.NBT.4	
Grade:	5
Domain:	Number and Operations in Base Ten
Cluster:	Understand the place value system.
Standard:	Use place value understanding to round decimals to any place.

Write a three-digit number and a two-digit number. Solve for the product of your two numbers using the standard algorithm. Explain, step-by-step, how you used the standard algorithm.

12 CCSS.5.NBT.5

1 Point

Answers will vary. Student must accurately show the product of the two numbers.

1 Point

Answers will vary. Student's explanation must be accurate and complete.

Total = 2 Points

Common Core State Standards for Mathematics 5.NBT.5	
Grade:	5
Domain:	Number and Operations in Base Ten
Cluster:	Perform operations with multi-digit whole numbers and with decimals to hundredths.
Standard:	Fluently multiply multi-digit whole numbers using the standard algorithm.

© Common Core Education, Inc.

Write a four-digit dividend. Use 12 as your divisor. Solve for the quotient. Draw a model using your knowledge of base ten or a rectangular array to show how you calculated your quotient.

CCSS.5.NBT.6 13

1 Point

Answers will vary. Student must accurately show the quotient of the two numbers.

1 Point

Student's model must illustrate the division problem written above.

Total = 2 Points

© Common Core Education, Inc.

Common Core State Standards for Mathematics 5.NBT.6	
Grade:	5
Domain:	Number and Operations in Base Ten
Cluster:	Perform operations with multi-digit whole numbers and with decimals to hundredths.
Standard:	Find whole-number quotients of whole numbers with up to four-digit dividends and two-digit divisors, using strategies based on place value, the properties of operations, and/or the relationship between multiplication and division. Illustrate and explain the calculation by using equations, rectangular arrays, and/or area models.

Solve for the difference between 121.1 and 10.29 using a place value strategy. **Draw** a model to represent the equation. **Explain** your use of the place value strategy.

14 CCSS.5.NBT.7—A

1 Point

110.81

1 Point

Student's model must accurately represent the equation.

1 Point

Answers will vary. Student's explanation must be accurate and complete.

Total = 3 Points

Common Core State Standards for Mathematics 5.NBT.7	
Grade:	5
Domain:	Number and Operations in Base Ten
Cluster:	Perform operations with multi-digit whole numbers and with decimals to hundredths.
Standard:	Add, subtract, multiply, and divide decimals to hundredths, using concrete models or drawings and strategies based on place value, properties of operations, and/or the relationship between addition and subtraction; relate the strategy to a written method and explain the reasoning used.

© Common Core Education, Inc.

Solve for the product of 284.62 and 1.5 using a place value strategy. Draw a model to represent the equation. Explain your use of the place value strategy.

CCSS.5.NBT.7—B 15

1 Point

426.930

1 Point

Student's model must accurately represent the equation.

1 Point

Answers will vary. Student's explanation must be accurate and complete.

Total = 3 Points

© Common Core Education, Inc.

Common Core State Standards for Mathematics 5.NBT.7	
Grade:	5
Domain:	Number and Operations in Base Ten
Cluster:	Perform operations with multi-digit whole numbers and with decimals to hundredths.
Standard:	Add, subtract, multiply, and divide decimals to hundredths, using concrete models or drawings and strategies based on place value, properties of operations, and/or the relationship between addition and subtraction; relate the strategy to a written method and explain the reasoning used.

Solve for the quotient of 576.35 divided by 5 using place value strategy. **Draw** a model to represent the equation. **Explain** your use of the place value strategy.

16 CCSS.5.NBT.7—C

1 Point

115.27

1 Point

Student's model must accurately represent the equation.

1 Point

Answers will vary. Student's explanation must be accurate and complete.

Total = 3 Points

Common Core State Standards for Mathematics 5.NBT.7	
Grade:	5
Domain:	Number and Operations in Base Ten
Cluster:	Perform operations with multi-digit whole numbers and with decimals to hundredths.
Standard:	Add, subtract, multiply, and divide decimals to hundredths, using concrete models or drawings and strategies based on place value, properties of operations, and/or the relationship between addition and subtraction; relate the strategy to a written method and explain the reasoning used.

© Common Core Education, Inc.

Write a mixed number. **Write** a fraction with a different denominator. **Explain** how you would add these two fractions. **Solve** for the sum.

CCSS.5.NF.1 17

1 Point

Answers will vary.

1 Point

Answers will vary. Student's explanation must include the use of a common denominator.

1 Point

Answers will vary.

Total = 3 Points

© Common Core Education, Inc.

Common Core State Standards for Mathematics 5.NF.1	
Grade:	5
Domain:	Number and Operations—Fractions
Cluster:	Use equivalent fractions as a strategy to add and subtract fractions.
Standard:	Add and subtract fractions with unlike denominators (including mixed numbers) by replacing given fractions with equivalent fractions in such a way as to produce an equivalent sum or difference of fractions with like denominators. *For example, 2/3 + 5/4 = 8/12 + 15/12 = 23/12. (In general, a/b + c/d = (ad + ac/bd).*

Write a word problem for the expression: $\frac{7}{8} - \frac{3}{4}$ **Draw** a model to represent the problem. **Solve** for the difference.

18 CCSS.5.NF.2

1 Point

Answers will vary. Question must be written accurately to receive full credit.

1 Point

Student's model must accurately illustrate the problem. Fraction models must be the same shape and the same size.

1 Point

1/8

Total = 3 Points

Common Core State Standards for Mathematics 5.NF.2	
Grade:	5
Domain:	Number and Operations—Fractions
Cluster:	Use equivalent fractions as a strategy to add and subtract fractions.
Standard:	Solve word problems involving addition and subtractions of fractions referring to the same whole, including cases of unlike denominators, e.g., by using visual fraction models or equations to represent the problem. Use benchmark fractions and number sense of fractions to estimate mentally and assess the reasonableness of answers. *For example, recognize an incorrect result 2/5 + 1/2 = 3/7 by observing that 3/7 <1/2.*

© Common Core Education, Inc.

Write a word problem for the expression 6 ÷ 30. **Draw** a fraction model to represent the problem. **Solve** for the quotient.

CCSS.5.NF.3 19

<u>1 Point</u>

Answers will vary. Question must be written accurately to receive full credit.

<u>1 Point</u>

Student's model must accurately illustrate the problem. Fraction models must be the same shape and the same size.

<u>1 Point</u>

1/5

Total = 3 Points

Common Core State Standards for Mathematics 5.NF.3	
Grade:	5
Domain:	Number and Operations—Fractions
Cluster:	Apply and extend previous understandings of multiplication and division to multiply and divide fractions.
Standard:	Interpret a fraction as division of the numerator by the denominator (*a/b = a ÷ b*). Solve word problems involving division of whole numbers leading to answers in the form of fractions or mixed numbers, e.g., by using visual fraction models or equations to represent the problem. *For example, interpret 3/4 as the result of division 3 by 4, noting that 3/4 multiplied by 4 equals 3, and that when 3 wholes are shared equally among 4 people each person has a share of size 3/4. If 9 people want to share a 50-pound sack of rice equally by weight, how many pounds of rice should each person get? Between what two whole numbers does your answer lie?*

© Common Core Education, Inc.

Write a word problem for the expression $\frac{2}{5} \times 4$ **Draw** a model to represent the problem. **Solve** for the product.

20 CCSS.5.NF.4.a—A

1 Point

Answers will vary. Question must be written accurately to receive full credit.

1 Point

Student's model must accurately illustrate the problem. Fraction models must be the same shape and the same size.

1 Point

1-3/5

Total = 3 Points

Common Core State Standards for Mathematics 5.NF.4.a	
Grade:	5
Domain:	Number and Operations—Fractions
Cluster:	Apply and extend previous understandings of multiplication and division to multiply and divide fractions.
Standard:	Apply and extend previous understandings of multiplication to multiply a fraction or whole number by a fraction. a. Interpret the product *(a/b) x q* as *a* parts of a partition of *q* into *b* equal parts; equivalently, as the result of a sequence of operations *a x q ÷ b*. *For example, use a visual fraction model to show (2/3) x 4 = 8/3, and create a story context for this equation. Do the same with (2/3) x (4/5) = 8/15. (In general, (a/b) x (c/d) = ac/bd.)*

© Common Core Education, Inc.

Write a word problem for the expression $\frac{2}{3} \times \frac{3}{4}$ **Draw** a model to represent the problem. **Solve** for the product.

CCSS.5.NF.4.a—B 21

<u>1 Point</u>

Answers will vary. Question must be written accurately to receive full credit.

<u>1 Point</u>

Student's model must accurately illustrate the problem. Fraction models must be the same shape and the same size.

<u>1 Point</u>

1/2

Total = 3 Points

Common Core State Standards for Mathematics 5.NF.4.a	
Grade:	5
Domain:	Number and Operations—Fractions
Cluster:	Apply and extend previous understandings of multiplication and division to multiply and divide fractions.
Standard:	Apply and extend previous understandings of multiplication to multiply a fraction or whole number by a fraction. a. Interpret the product *(a/b) x q* as *a* parts of a partition of *q* into *b* equal parts; equivalently, as the result of a sequence of operations *a x q ÷ b*. *For example, use a visual fraction model to show (2/3) x 4 = 8/3, and create a story context for this equation. Do the same with (2/3) x (4/5) = 8/15. (In general, (a/b) x (c/d) = ac/bd.)*

© Common Core Education, Inc.

Draw a rectangle with side lengths measuring 1-1/2" by 3-3/4". **Solve** for the area by counting the square units. **Solve** for the area by multiplying the side lengths. **Explain** why these measurements are the same.

□ = 1/4" x 1/4"

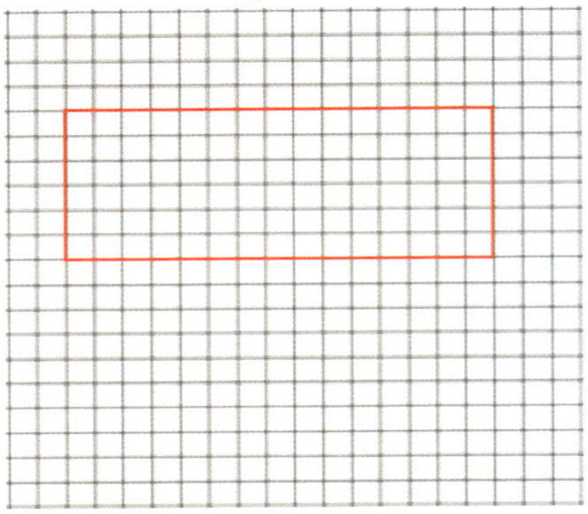

22 CCSS.5.NF.4.b

1 Point

Student's drawing is accurate. (See sample diagram at left.)

1 Point

60 sixteenth square units = 60/16 = 5-10/16 = 5-5/8 square units

1 Point

5-5/8 square units

1 Point

Answers will vary. Student's explanation must be accurate and complete.

Total = 4 Points

Common Core State Standards for Mathematics 5.NF.4.b	
Grade:	5
Domain:	Number and Operations—Fractions
Cluster:	Apply and extend previous understandings of multiplication and division to multiply and divide fractions.
Standard:	Apply and extend previous understandings of multiplication to multiply a fraction or whole number by a fraction. b. Find the area of a rectangle with fractional side lengths by tiling it with unit squares of the appropriate unit fraction side lengths, and show that the area is the same as would be found by multiplying the side lengths. Multiply fractional side lengths to find areas of rectangles, and represent fraction products as rectangular areas.

© Common Core Education, Inc.

Write a multiplication expression that includes a whole number and a fraction. **Solve** for the product. **Explain** why the product is less than the whole number factor.

CCSS.5.NF.5.a 23

1 Point

Answers will vary.

1 Point

Answers will vary.

1 Point

Answers will vary. Student's explanation must be accurate and complete.

Total = 3 Points

Common Core State Standards for Mathematics 5.NF.5.a	
Grade:	5
Domain:	Number and Operations—Fractions
Cluster:	Apply and extend previous understandings of multiplication and division to multiply and divide fractions.
Standard:	Interpret multiplication as scaling (resizing), by: a. Comparing the size of a product to the size of one factor on the basis of the size of the other factor, without performing the indicated multiplication.

© Common Core Education, Inc.

Write a multiplication expression that includes a whole number and a mixed number. **Solve** for the product. **Explain** why the product is greater than the whole number factor.

24 CCSS.5.NF.5.b

1 Point

Answers will vary.

1 Point

Answers will vary.

1 Point

Answers will vary. Student's explanation must be accurate and complete.

Total = 3 Points

Common Core State Standards for Mathematics 5.NF.5.b	
Grade:	5
Domain:	Number and Operations—Fractions
Cluster:	Apply and extend previous understandings of multiplication and division to multiply and divide fractions.
Standard:	Interpret multiplication as scaling (resizing), by: b. Explaining why multiplying a given number by a fraction greater than 1 results in a product greater than the given number (recognizing multiplication by whole numbers greater than 1 as a familiar case); explaining why multiplying a given number by a fraction less than 1 results in a product smaller than the given number; and relating the principle of fraction equivalence $a/b = (n \times a)/(n \times b)$ to the effect of multiplying a/b by 1.

© Common Core Education, Inc.

Write a multiplication expression involving fractions. Write a word problem for the expression. Draw a model to represent the problem. Solve for the product.

CCSS.5.NF.6 25

1 Point

Answers will vary.

1 Point

Answers will vary. Question must be written accurately to receive full credit.

1 Point

Fraction models must be the same shape and the same size.

1 Point

Answers will vary.

Total = 4 Points

© Common Core Education, Inc.

Common Core State Standards for Mathematics 5.NF.6	
Grade:	5
Domain:	Number and Operations—Fractions
Cluster:	Apply and extend previous understandings of multiplication and division to multiply and divide fractions.
Standard:	Solve real world problems involving multiplication of fractions and mixed numbers, e.g., by using visual fraction models or equations to represent the problem.

Write a word problem for the expression $\frac{1}{4} \div 3$ **Draw** a model to represent the problem. **Solve** for the quotient. **Write** a multiplication equation to check your work.

26 CCSS.5.NF.7.a

1 Point

Answers will vary. Question must be written accurately to receive full credit.

1 Point

Fraction models must be the same shape and the same size.

1 Point

1/12

1 Point

1/4 x 1/3 = 1/12

Total = 4 Points

Common Core State Standards for Mathematics 5.NF.7.a	
Grade:	5
Domain:	Number and Operations—Fractions
Cluster:	Apply and extend previous understandings of multiplication and division to multiply and divide fractions.
Standard:	Apply and extend previous understandings of division to divide unit fractions by whole numbers and whole numbers by unit fractions. a. Interpret division of a unit fraction by a non-zero whole number, and compute such quotients. *For example, create a story context for (1/3) ÷ 4, and use a visual fraction model to show the quotient. Use the relationship between multiplication and division to explain that (1/3) ÷ 4 = 1/12 because (1/12) x 4 = 1/3.*

© Common Core Education, Inc.

Write a word problem for the expression $5 \div \frac{1}{4}$ Draw a model to represent the problem. Solve for the quotient. Write a multiplication equation to check your work.

CCSS.5.NF.7.b 27

1 Point

Answers will vary. Question must be written accurately to receive full credit.

1 Point

Fraction models must be the same shape and the same size.

1 Point

20

1 Point

5/1 x 4/1 = 20

Total = 4 Points

Common Core State Standards for Mathematics 5.NF.7.b	
Grade:	5
Domain:	Number and Operations—Fractions
Cluster:	Apply and extend previous understandings of multiplication and division to multiply and divide fractions.
Standard:	Apply and extend previous understandings of division to divide unit fractions by whole numbers and whole numbers by unit fractions. b. Interpret division of a whole number by a unit fraction, and compute such quotients. *For example, create a story context for 4 ÷ (1/5), and use a visual fraction model to show the quotient. Use the relationship between multiplication and division to explain that 4 ÷ (1/5) = 20 because 20 x (1/5) = 4.*

© Common Core Education, Inc.

Write an expression with a fraction dividend and a whole number divisor. Write a word problem for the expression. Solve for the quotient. Write a multiplication equation to check your work.

28 CCSS.5.NF.7.c—A

<u>1 Point</u>

Answers will vary.

<u>1 Point</u>

Answers will vary. Question must be written accurately to receive full credit.

<u>1 Point</u>

Answers will vary.

<u>1 Point</u>

Answers will vary.

Total = 4 Points

Common Core State Standards for Mathematics 5.NF.7.c	
Grade:	5
Domain:	Number and Operations—Fractions
Cluster:	Apply and extend previous understandings of multiplication and division to multiply and divide fractions.
Standard:	Apply and extend previous understandings of division to divide unit fractions by whole numbers and whole numbers by unit fractions. c. Solve real world problems involving division of unit fractions by non-zero whole numbers and division of whole numbers by unit fractions, e.g., by using visual fraction models and equations to represent the problem. *For example, how much chocolate will each person get if 3 people share 1/2 lb of chocolate equally? How many 1/3-cup servings are in 2 cups of raisins?*

© Common Core Education, Inc.

Write an expression with a whole number dividend and a fraction divisor. Write a word problem for the expression. Solve for the quotient. Write a multiplication equation to check your work.

1 Point

Answers will vary.

1 Point

Answers will vary. Question must be written accurately to receive full credit.

1 Point

Answers will vary.

1 Point

Answers will vary.

CCSS.5.NF.7.c—B 29

Total = 4 Points

Common Core State Standards for Mathematics 5.NF.7.c	
Grade:	5
Domain:	Number and Operations—Fractions
Cluster:	Apply and extend previous understandings of multiplication and division to multiply and divide fractions.
Standard:	Apply and extend previous understandings of division to divide unit fractions by whole numbers and whole numbers by unit fractions. c. Solve real world problems involving division of unit fractions by non-zero whole numbers and division of whole numbers by unit fractions, e.g., by using visual fraction models and equations to represent the problem. *For example, how much chocolate will each person get if 3 people share 1/2 lb of chocolate equally? How many 1/3-cup servings are in 2 cups of raisins?*

© Common Core Education, Inc.

Explain how to find the number of pints in one gallon. **Draw** a picture to support your explanation. **Write** an example of when you might need to convert measurements in the real world.

30 CCSS.5.MD.1

1 Point

Answers will vary. Student's explanation must be accurate and complete.

1 Point

Student's drawing must accurately illustrate the explanation.

1 Point

Answers will vary but must be reasonable.

Total = 3 Points

Common Core State Standards for Mathematics 5.MD.1	
Grade:	5
Domain:	Measurement and Data
Cluster:	Convert like measurement units within a given measurement system.
Standard:	Convert among different-sized standard measurement units within a given measurement system (e.g., convert 5 cm to 0.05 m), and use these conversions in solving multi-step, real world problems.

© Common Core Education, Inc.

Draw a line plot that includes the following data. Include a title for your line plot.

$2\frac{1}{8}$ $1\frac{1}{4}$ $\frac{1}{8}$ $2\frac{1}{8}$ $1\frac{1}{2}$ $\frac{1}{8}$ $1\frac{1}{2}$ $2\frac{1}{8}$ $1\frac{3}{4}$ $2\frac{3}{4}$

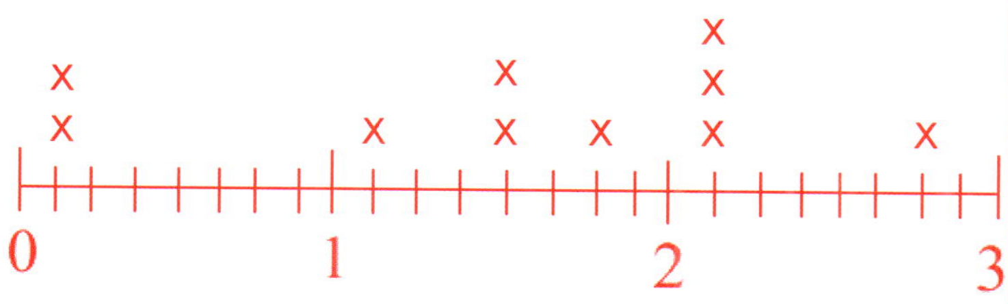

1 Point

See example at left.

Write a multiplication or division question that could be asked using the data in your line plot. **Solve** for the answer.

1 Point

Answers will vary. Question must be written accurately to receive full credit.

1 Point

Answers will vary.

CCSS.5.MD.2 31

Total = 3 Points

Common Core State Standards for Mathematics 5.MD.2	
Grade:	5
Domain:	Measurement and Data
Cluster:	Represent and interpret data.
Standard:	Make a line plot to display a data set of measurements in fractions and a unit (1/2, 1/4, 18). Use operations on fractions for this grade to solve problems involving information presented in line plots. *For example, given different measurements of liquid in identical beakers, find the amount of liquid each beaker would contain if the total amount in all the beakers were redistributed equally.*

© Common Core Education, Inc.

Write the possible dimensions of a rectangular prism with a volume of 48 cubic units. **Explain** how you could change the dimensions of the rectangular prism without changing the volume.

32 CCSS.5.MD.3.a

1 Point

Student writes one of these possible dimensions:

2 x 4 x 6
3 x 2 x 8
1 x 2 x 24
1 x 4 x 12
1 x 6 x 8

1 Point

Answers will vary. Student's explanation must include other possible dimensions.

Total = 2 Points

Common Core State Standards for Mathematics 5.MD.3.a	
Grade:	5
Domain:	Measurement and Data
Cluster:	Geometric measurement: understand concepts of volume and relate volume to multiplication and to addition.
Standard:	Recognize volume as an attribute of solid figures and understand concepts of volume measurement. a. A cube with side length 1 unit, called a "unit cube," is said to have "one cubic unit" of volume, and can be used to measure volume.

© Common Core Education, Inc.

Explain how you would measure the volume of a box using cubic units.

CCSS.5.MD.3.b 33

1 Point

Answers will vary. Student's explanation must show an understanding of volume.

Total = 1 Points

© Common Core Education, Inc.

Common Core State Standards for Mathematics 5.MD.3.b	
Grade:	5
Domain:	Measurement and Data
Cluster:	Geometric measurement: understand concepts of volume and relate volume to multiplication and to addition.
Standard:	Recognize volume as an attribute of solid figures and understand concepts of volume measurement. b. A solid figure which can be packed without gaps or overlaps using *n* unit cubes is said to have a volume of *n* cubic units.

Write an example of what you could measure using cubic centimeters.

1 Point

Answers will vary but must be reasonable.

Write an example of what you could measure using cubic feet.

1 Point

Answers will vary but must be reasonable.

Write an example of what you could measure using cubic meters.

1 Point

Answers will vary but must be reasonable.

Explain a situation in which you would use improvised units to measure volume.

1 Point

Answers will vary but must be reasonable.

34 CCSS.5.MD.4

Total = 4 Points

Common Core State Standards for Mathematics 5.MD.4	
Grade:	5
Domain:	Measurement and Data
Cluster:	Geometric measurement: understand concepts of volume and relate volume to multiplication and to addition.
Standard:	Measure volumes by counting unit cubes, using cubic cm, cubic in, cubic ft, and improvised units.

© Common Core Education, Inc.

Explain why the formula Volume = length x width x height works for finding the volume of rectangular prisms.

1 Point

Answers will vary. Student's explanation must be accurate and complete.

Explain whether this formula could be used to find the volume of a can of juice.

1 Point

No. Student's explanation must be accurate and complete.

CCSS.5.MD.5.a 35

Total = 2 Points

Common Core State Standards for Mathematics 5.MD.5.a	
Grade:	5
Domain:	Measurement and Data
Cluster:	Geometric measurement: understand concepts of volume and relate volume to multiplication and to addition.
Standard:	Relate volume to the operations of multiplication and addition and solve real world and mathematical problems involving volume. a. Find the volume of a right rectangular prism with whole-number side lengths by packing it with unit cubes, and show that the volume is the same as would be found by multiplying the edge lengths, equivalently by multiplying the height by the area of the base. Represent threefold whole-number products as volumes, e.g., to represent the associative property of multiplication.

© Common Core Education, Inc.

Write a word problem in which you would have to solve for the volume of a rectangular prism. Solve your word problem using a formula.

36 CCSS.5.MD.5.b

1 Point

Answers will vary. Question must be written accurately to receive full credit.

1 Point

Answers will vary but student must use a formula.

Total = 2 Points

Common Core State Standards for Mathematics 5.MD.5.b	
Grade:	5
Domain:	Measurement and Data
Cluster:	Geometric measurement: understand concepts of volume and relate volume to multiplication and to addition.
Standard:	Relate volume to the operations of multiplication and addition and solve real world and mathematical problems involving volume. b. Apply the formulas $V = l \times w \times h$ and $V = b \times h$ for rectangular prisms to find volumes of right rectangular prisms with whole-number edge lengths in the context of solving real world and mathematical problems.

© Common Core Education, Inc.

Zayden needs to buy one container to pack and ship two identical boxes. The dimensions of each box is 2 inches by 4 inches by 8 inches.

Solve for the dimensions and the volume of the smallest container Zayden can buy to pack and ship his boxes. (Hint: Make sure both boxes can fit within the dimensions of the container.) **Explain** how you solved this problem.

CCSS.5.MD.5.c 37

1 Point

128 cubic inches

4 in x 4 in x 8 in

2 in x 8 in x 8 in

2 in x 4 in x 16 in

1 Point

Answers will vary. Student's explanation must be accurate and complete.

Total = 2 Points

Common Core State Standards for Mathematics 5.MD.5.c	
Grade:	5
Domain:	Measurement and Data
Cluster:	Geometric measurement: understand concepts of volume and relate volume to multiplication and to addition.
Standard:	Relate volume to the operations of multiplication and addition and solve real world and mathematical problems involving volume. c. Recognize volume as additive. Find volumes of solid figures composed of two non-overlapping right rectangular prisms by adding the volumes of the non-overlapping parts, applying this technique to solve real world problems.

© Common Core Education, Inc.

Draw a coordinate system with an origin of zero. **Label** the *x*-axis and *y*-axis with intervals of 1. **Plot** (7, 10). **Explain** how you plotted the coordinates.

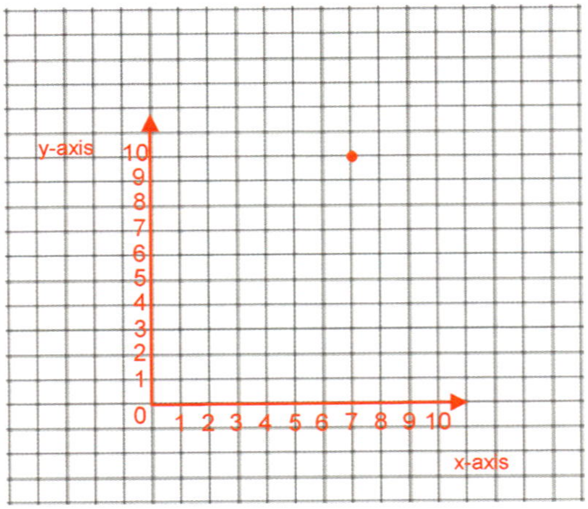

1 Point

See example at left.

1 Point

Answers will vary. Student's explanation must be accurate and complete.

38 CCSS.5.G.1

Total = 2 Points

Common Core State Standards for Mathematics 5.G.1	
Grade:	5
Domain:	Geometry
Cluster:	Graph points on the coordinate plane to solve real-world and mathematical problems.
Standard:	Use a pair of perpendicular number lines, called axes, to define a coordinate system, with the intersection of the lines (the origin) arranged to coincide with the 0 on each line and a given point in the plane located by using an ordered pair of numbers, called its coordinates. Understand that the first number indicates how far to travel from the origin in the direction of one axis, and the second number indicates how far to travel in the direction of the second axis, with the convention that the names of the two axes and the coordinates correspond (e.g., *x*-axis and *x*-coordinate, *y*-axis and *y*-coordinate).

© Common Core Education, Inc.

Draw a coordinate system with an origin of zero. Label the x-axis and y-axis with intervals of 1.

Jan's house is located at (7, 8). **Plot** and label Jan's house on the coordinate grid. The post office is located six blocks west and three blocks south of Jan's house. **Plot** and label the post office. **Explain** how many blocks Jan will travel from her house to the post office if she travels the most efficient way.

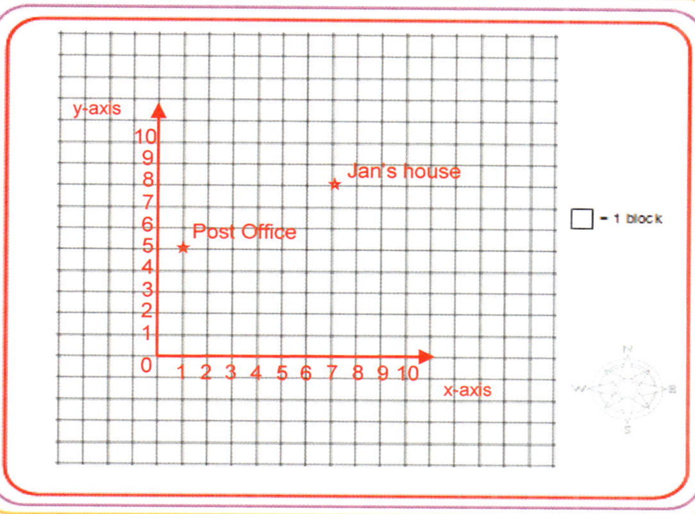

1 Point

See example at left.

1 Point

Answers will vary. Student's explanation must be accurate and complete.

CCSS.5.G.2 39

Total = 2 Points

© Common Core Education, Inc.

Common Core State Standards for Mathematics 5.G.2	
Grade:	5
Domain:	Geometry
Cluster:	Graph points on the coordinate plane to solve real-world and mathematical problems.
Standard:	Represent real world and mathematical problems by graphing points in the first quadrant of the coordinate plane, and interpret coordinate values of points in the context of the situation.

Write all the attributes of a rectangle. **Write** two other ways you can classify a rectangle. **Explain** your classifications.

40 CCSS.5.G.3

1 Point

4 sides
4 right angles
2 pairs of parallel lines
2 pairs of congruent sides

1 Point

Parallelogram
Quadrilateral

1 Point

Answers will vary. Student's explanation must be accurate and complete.

Total = 3 Points

Common Core State Standards for Mathematics 5.G.3	
Grade:	5
Domain:	Geometry
Cluster:	Classify two-dimensional figures into categories based on their properties.
Standard:	Understand that attributes belonging to a category of two-dimensional figures also belong to all subcategories of that category. *For example, all rectangles have four right angles and squares are rectangles, so all squares have four right angles.*

© Common Core Education, Inc.

Write the hierarchy of quadrilateral to square. **Explain** the hierarchy using the attributes of each figure.

CCSS.5.G.4 41

1 Point

Quadrilateral > parallelogram > rectangle > square

1 Point

Answers will vary. Student's explanation must be accurate and complete.

Total = 2 Points

© Common Core Education, Inc.

Common Core State Standards for Mathematics 5.G.4	
Grade:	5
Domain:	Geometry
Cluster:	Classify two-dimensional figures into categories based on their properties.
Standard:	Classify two-dimensional figures in a hierarchy based on properties.

© Common Core Education, Inc.

Content Vocabulary Prompts

© Common Core Education, Inc.

Multiplication

Draw a picture or model that shows **multiplication**. Label your picture or model. **Explain** what **multiplication** means.

44 5.CV.1

1 Point

Student's picture or model

1 Point

Student's picture or model is correctly labeled with an

1 Point

Student's explanation includes "multiplication" as you have

Total = 3 Points

Content Vocabulary 5.CV.1	
Grades:	3, 4, 5
Term:	Multiplication
Gr. 5 CCSS Critical Area Alignment:	(1) Developing fluency with addition and subtraction of fractions, and developing understanding of the multiplication of fractions and of division of fractions in limited cases (unit fractions divided by whole numbers and whole numbers divided by unit fractions).

© Common Core Education, Inc.

Division

Draw a picture or model that shows **division**. Label your picture or model. Explain what **division** means.

5.CV.2 45

1 Point

Student's picture or model represents division.

1 Point

Student's picture or model is correctly labeled with an equation.

1 Point

Student's explanation includes "division" as you have defined it in your class.

Total = 3 Points

Content Vocabulary 5.CV.2	
Grades:	3, 4, 5
Term:	Division
Gr. 5 CCSS Critical Area Alignment:	(1) Developing fluency with addition and subtraction of fractions, and developing understanding of the multiplication of fractions and of division of fractions in limited cases (unit fractions divided by whole numbers and whole numbers divided by unit fractions). (2) Extending division to 2-digit divisors, integrating decimal fractions into the place value system and developing understanding of operations with decimals to hundredths, and developing fluency with whole number and decimal operations.

© Common Core Education, Inc.

Expression—Equation

Write a multiplication or division **expression** using a symbol to represent an unknown number.

← 1 Point

Answers will vary.

Write a multiplication or division **equation** using a symbol to represent an unknown number.

← 1 Point

Answers will vary.

Explain the similarities and differences between an **expression** and an **equation**.

← 1 Point

Answers will vary. Student's explanation includes "expression" and "equation" as you have defined it in your class.

46 5.CV.3

Total = 3 Points

Content Vocabulary 5.CV.3	
Grades:	1, 2, 3, 4, 5 (Equation) 5 (Expression)
Term:	Expression—Equation
Gr. 5 CCSS Critical Area Alignment:	N/A

© Common Core Education, Inc.

Decimal

Write a **decimal** with value in the hundredths place. **Draw** a picture or a model to represent your **decimal**. What is a **decimal**? **Explain**.

5.CV.4 47

1 Point

Answers will vary.

1 Point

Answers will vary. Student's drawing must accurately represent the decimal written.

1 Point

Student's explanation includes "decimal" as you have defined it in class.

Total = 3 Points

© Common Core Education, Inc.

Content Vocabulary 5.CV.4	
Grades:	4, 5
Term:	Decimal
Gr. 5 CCSS Critical Area Alignment:	(2) Extending division to 2-digit divisors, integrating decimal fractions into the place value system and developing understanding of operations with decimals to hundredths, and developing fluency with whole number and decimal operations.

Fraction

Write a **fraction**. **Draw** a picture or model to represent your **fraction**.
Explain the parts of a **fraction** and what they represent.

48 5.CV.5

<u>1 Point</u>

Answers will vary.

<u>1 Point</u>

Student's drawing accurately represents the fraction written.

<u>1 Point</u>

Student's explanation includes "fraction" as you have defined it in class.

Total = 3 Points

Content Vocabulary 5.CV.5	
Grades:	3, 4, 5
Term:	Fraction
Gr. 5 CCSS Critical Area Alignment:	(1) Developing fluency with addition and subtraction of fractions, and developing understanding of the multiplication of fractions and of division of fractions in limited cases (unit fractions divided by whole numbers and whole numbers divided by unit fractions).

© Common Core Education, Inc.

Mixed Number

Write a **mixed number**. **Draw** a picture or model to represent your **mixed number**. **Explain** the parts of a **mixed number** and what they represent.

5.CV6 49

1 Point

Answers will vary.

1 Point

Answers will vary. Student's drawing must accurately represent the mixed number written.

1 Point

Student's explanation includes "mixed number" as you have defined it in class.

Total = 3 Points

© Common Core Education, Inc.

Content Vocabulary 5.CV.6	
Grades:	4, 5
Term:	Mixed Number
Gr. 5 CCSS Critical Area Alignment:	(1) Developing fluency with addition and subtraction of fractions, and developing understanding of the multiplication of fractions and of division of fractions in limited cases (unit fractions divided by whole numbers and whole numbers divided by unit fractions).

Equivalent Fractions

Write a set of **equivalent fractions**. **Draw** a picture or model to represent your **fractions**. What are **equivalent fractions**? **Explain**.

50 5.CV.7

1 Point

Student writes an equivalent fraction.

1 Point

Student's drawing accurately represents the fractions written. Fraction models must be the same shape and the same size.

1 Point

Answers will vary. Student's explanation includes "equivalent fractions" as you have defined them in class.

Total = 3 Points

Content Vocabulary 5.CV.7	
Grades:	5
Term:	Equivalent Fractions
Gr. 5 CCSS Critical Area Alignment:	(1) Developing fluency with addition and subtraction of fractions, and developing understanding of the multiplication of fractions and of division of fractions in limited cases (unit fractions divided by whole numbers and whole numbers divided by unit fractions).

© Common Core Education, Inc.

Area

Draw an example of an **area** model or array. What is **area**? **Explain**. **Write** two examples of when you would need to find **area** in the real world.

5.CV.8 51

1 Point

Student accurately draws an area model or array.

1 Point

Student's explanation includes "area" as you have defined it in class.

2 Points

Student writes two real world examples of when area would need to be found. (1 point for each example)

Total = 4 Points

© Common Core Education, Inc.

Content Vocabulary 5.CV.8	
Grades:	3, 4, 5
Term:	Area
Gr. 5 CCSS Critical Area Alignment:	N/A

Volume

Draw 3 items that have **volume**. Label your items with the item name. What is **volume**? Explain.

52 5.CV.9

3 Points

Student's drawing includes 3 labeled items that have volume (1 point for each term).

1 Point

Student's explanation includes "volume" as you have defined it in your class.

Total = 4 Points

Content Vocabulary 5.CV.9	
Grades:	3, 4, 5
Term:	Volume
Gr. 5 CCSS Critical Area Alignment:	(3) Developing understanding of volume.

© Common Core Education, Inc.

Data

Write an example of **data** that you could collect from your classmates. What is **data**? **Explain.**

5.CV.10 53

<u>1 Point</u>

Student writes an example of data that could be collected from classmates.

<u>1 Point</u>

Student's explanation includes "data" as you have defined it in your class.

Total = 2 Points

© Common Core Education, Inc.

Content Vocabulary 5.CV.10	
Grades:	1, 2, 3, 4, 5
Term:	Data
Gr. 5 CCSS Critical Area Alignment:	N/A

Solid Figure

Draw and label 3 examples of **solid figures**. What is a **solid figure**? Explain.

54 5.CV.11

3 Points

Student's drawing includes 3 labeled solid figures.

1 Point

Answers will vary. Student's explanation includes "solid figure" as you have defined it in your class.

Total = 4 Points

© Common Core Education, Inc.

Content Vocabulary 5.CV.11	
Grades:	1, 5 (Solid Figure) 2 (Three-dimensional Shape)
Term:	Solid Figure
Gr. 5 CCSS Critical Area Alignment:	(3) Developing understanding of volume.

Attribute

Draw and label a solid figure. Write the **attributes** of your solid figure. What is an **attribute**? Explain.

5.CV.12 55

1 Point

Student accurately draws and labels a solid figure.

1 Point

Student writes the attributes of the shape drawn.

1 Point

Answers will vary. Student's explanation includes "attribute" as you have defined it in class.

Total = 3 Points

© Common Core Education, Inc.

Content Vocabulary 5.CV.12	
Grades:	3, 4 (Property) 5 (Attribute)
Term:	Attribute
Gr. 5 CCSS Critical Area Alignment:	N/A

Two-dimensional Figure

Draw and label 3 examples of **two-dimensional figures**. What is a **two-dimensional figure**? **Explain.**

56 5.CV.13

<u>3 Points</u>

Student's drawing includes 3 labeled two-dimensional figures.

<u>1 Point</u>

Answers will vary. Student's explanation includes "two-dimensional figure" as you have defined it in your class.

Total = 4 Points

Content Vocabulary 5.CV.13	
Grades:	1 (Plane Figure) 2, 5 (Two-dimensional Figure)
Term:	Two-dimensional Figure
Gr. 5 CCSS Critical Area Alignment:	N/A

© Common Core Education, Inc.

Coordinate Plane

Draw and label a **coordinate plane**. **Explain** step by step how to graph points on a **coordinate plane**.

5.CV.14 57

1 Points

Student's drawing is accurate and complete.

1 Point

Answers will vary. Student's explanation is accurate and complete.

Total = 2 Points

© Common Core Education, Inc.

Content Vocabulary 5.CV.14	
Grades:	5
Term:	Coordinate Plane
Gr. 5 CCSS Critical Area Alignment:	N/A

25348208R00040

Made in the USA
Charleston, SC
22 December 2013